Cigarette in Hand

A miscellany of poesy

By: David Horowitz

For my mother

The karaoke singer

That song
        That
    Song.

He sings
    He sings

Could he make Emil Cioran repeat his maxim
With
        The opening lines

Of that DAMNED SONG

(2016)

He looks different

he is much different than what I expected
At least,
       I know him
  N o w

But is he the person I never knew?

(2016)

Divinity

You often accuse me
But you

Deny it

You have not want of anything

It is still a wonderful time, for it

Is normal

So
They say

Divinity is nothing without
Base desire

(2016)

I am so sorry

I always seem to do something wrong

I seem
To
Always
Do
This

Why can I never be able to
Do
What's right

I always miss the mark
I forget to double check

Stress

Stress
Stress

Sorry

Apology

Accept it because
I want you to be happy

Stress
Stress
Stress

Let us be happy

(2016)

Work

We all try to

HIDE

When   We

Are supposed to

W
O
R
K

(2016)

Vegan

i try to keep steadfast

I try (I do)
But it is *paris*
What can I do? (This is a chance
I might not)
Get.   Again.

It is not like we can have a margret d'un orange
To, I am sure it would be good too

I can't wait to go back to
Being vegan

(2016)

Le bus

paris has a night bus that takes you far away
It comes not when the sun shines its very ray
              I wish I could always be here
paris is able to host every bit of the world
              The bus shows you it first hand

A ticket is 1€90

                         Get on

                         (2016)

Jacques Bonsergent

We walk for miles up stairs
Métro
Métro

Droite   *Gauche*

Je me sens

I just hold on to the bar
I just want to sit down and
Open
My
Book

This morning we took a train to the south
We dined with Napoleon
Marie-Antoinette was here

I just sit here now
At JB
I wish I could just be at the boulangerie

(2016)

Gare des Moules

I sit here after changing tables
I hear the soft music above me
The buses come and go
Tabasco sauce and limes
The bread is *à table*
Paris is everything
Yet, Belgium seems near

I just wish could stay with *La Marinière*
I don't want to leave
I want to stay forever
At this very

Corner

(2016)

Leaving Paris

Why must we go?
When there is a whole world
Within

I cannot help but notice that you were
Happier
Here
Than anywhere else

People say to do what makes you
Happy
Let us go then, you and I
To touch the very Parisian sky
And stay here e'er after we die

Why much this train go so swiftly?
Can it not just stay in its place
I have no need to leave
Nor no need to race

I see the turbines
And my Gallimard book
We are the salt of the earth
Paris

Paris

(2016)

Le feu follet

Alain, you remind with me forever
If I'd never met you
Where would I be?

The stench of not having changed in days
The aroma of old, worn books
My bag with everything I need to live

The fire burns as it wisps away
The piano fills the still air
Aid me now
As I take this drink

(2016)

Salt

Where are you going?
Île Saint-Louis
Where are you from?
Île de la Cité

If only Bastille wasn't so far from here
I have to get to Républic
I see him!
I see him!

Renée is with him

(2016)

Terre

A spire fills the sky with the dark grey
Of humanity
The trees abound past the golden fields
Brick
Brick
Stone
Brick

Another forest

A wall of verdure

Gold upon brown

Or sur la terre

(2016)

À Londres

London is a city
Not very from here

Yet, every time I see it
I feel the need for fear

Howards End taught me
The city is a sneeze
It grows like weeds with heat
And never has a cooling breeze

Where are they?
The Wilcoxes
I am he, Mr. Bast

(2016)

Too Late

I always punctual
Except for this one thing
I was so late

I suffer because of it
Because it makes me

Less

For once, being early would've been best
Or was I fashionably late?
No,

This is not something one can be
Late to.

I guess I will be punished for being

Tardy

(2016)

Tashkent

        I knew you were

          Just

Another

        Count Vronsky

       Maybe I should have
       Gone to Tashkent

It would have been best
         Instead,

      I am Levin

      (2016)

Samarqand

Sitting on the canal
The turquoise domes
The heat of summer abounds
I hear the calls

Persian
Arabic

The muezzin calls

What will this city be
Moments from now?

I can't imagine how I will feel
Once I leave the city walls

Of Samarqand

(2016)

Damascus

Do you remember where we met?
Overlooking Damascus
We looked up at the stars
Like him

I looked into your eyes
And there, I saw a universe
All its own

Now, atop the mount I am again
With your lips on mine
But you're no longer here

In
Damascus

(2016)

Kazan

We spent our youth
Searching for love
In the brothels

We found friends
Women who accepted us

As we made love
To all those men
Who also came here looking
For something
Resembling

Love

Kazan was different
Our outstretched arms
In the summer sun

Wheat fields stretch
As far as our eyes can see

Take me back to that brothel
Where we fell in love

(2016)

Symrna

The jewish man
Is dead

The carpet man
Is dead

The Hindoo man
Is dead

Yet, Homer is still alive

(2016)

Persepolis

We had sex
With russians
Because

They

Gave us

A book of sand

(2016)

Moscow

Tehran is sprawling
The fountains flow

They retreat in the mountain

Where the waterfall flows
To the
Meat shop

(2016)

Methuselah

Do you remember?
When you tortured me

You said it was normal
To feel pain

Agony

Depression

Because you said
It made you happy

(2016)

Mr. Maze

He was one of twins
His eyes were so green

He drank hot milk before bed
Because he knew he couldn't sleep
Otherwise

Other wise

He knew nothing
Because he knew

Nothing contains everything

(2016)

Jameson

Beaches are not good places for
People who hate

Irrational irritation

Jameson Pointe was the site

Where hatred took its toll

Will they ever find the body

?

(2016)

Around the lake

You fucked him
In the cave by the lake

To believe
You were on my lap as you did it

I saw everything
Because I had nothing

You looked at me as you did it
Telling me I was going

To have to walk you back home
Since your parents were away

We held hands
As we walked down the hill

We found the homeless guy
And we crawled into his tent

Ohell
Ohell

You fucked him too

Because there was nothing else to do

(2016)

Devon

We sipped tea
And
Spread
Devonshire cream

"So what is his name again?
Devon, right?"

(2016)

George

The Germans loved you
Because you were
A Russophile

Hegel
Bach

If only I had met you
Before

You were born

(2016)

Mixy

It isn't infectious for humans

"But all I want to do is die."

(2016)

Das Neue Welt

Duets are for people
Who skin themselves alive

We can't all be named Sebastian

(2016)

The Maltese Nights

You went there for
Research purposes

I learnt a lot from your study

You were right

If only I could thank you

I learnt more from one conversation
Than in all a semester of lectures

You were right

I even imagined
Attending another class
Of yours

You went to Malta
And spent your nights
Hard at study
Of every man's body

I wish I could have

As much of a repository of knowledge
Like you

(2016)

Scheherezade

One thousand and one nights
I shall give you

Once they are done

Our story

Will

End

(2016)

Melpomene

O Muse

Where are you
When I need

Nothing but

TRAGEDY

(2016)

Queen

                    Rani
                    Rani
                    Rani

                    Stay
Away   From   That

                    Fish

                    (2016)

Gingersnaps

I remember Texas afternoons
We sat there watching the rain as it came
Across the plains

Lemonade
Sweet Tea
And Gingersnaps

I would stare at the sky
As gilded streams
Fell upon the Earth

The sound of the tornado sirens
The sound of the leaves falling

Perfect bliss

A perfect summer's day

(2016)

On the sight of the moon

O ISRAEL

to think we have seen this moon
From

Every angle
On the Earth

(2016)

21

Being this age
I have done
Nothing
That I *wanted* to have done

By now

Still

21

Is better than being 22

And dead to society

(2016)

Au Café

Here I am again
Sitting with my head upon my hand
Au café
Somewhere to stay, all day

I sit listening to all the life around me
And I think about my own

To think, this is the best way
To get to know yourself

I stare into the city as it moves
As I move not a single inch

This is where I am most myself
In a café
Sipping
Au Lait

(2016)

Marcus Antonius

Rome remembers you
A living god

I am Cleopatra
Who was dragged through the
Streets of your city

I should've slept in a
Bed of snakes

To escape you.

(2016)

St. Petersburg

I wanted it
That is what I told myself
Night
After
Night
After night

I should've let it happen
More
And again

Since, I deserved it.

(2016)

Lemons

Remember when we were in
Our clubhouse

We would take lemons from the tree
And make it into lemonade

We would press our
Chilled lips together

And smile.

(2016)

Ryuk

I wish I could be like you
Because
You are all I ever wanted to be

A *shinigami*

All I want is to be in your world
I would have the power
To create beauty,
Everywhere I go

(2016)

Thousands of Hours

I have spent so much time
Looking for perfection
I saw it
Every time I scrolled down

Thousands of hours
Through a museum of beauty

Only one portrait was worthless

Mine.

(2016)

Complications

No strings attached
To everything
Is what you wanted

I still ready your message
Every
Single
Day

But, of course, here
I am.

(2016)

Truth

Truth is
Nothing

To some who
Has only
Fictions
To live

(2016)

Dites-Moi

What am I to tell you?

You already know

Why?
Why?
Why?

(2016)

Hold Me

When you hold me
I feel like I am
Somewhere
I can finally call home

I have never had a home
Until your arms wrapped around me

Hold me
Hold me

I want to cry when we are apart

I know people will say
It is what children do

But children know what is
Innocent love

Our love is so innocent
So pure
And so full

Hold me
Hold me

What I would give
For your arms
To always be around me

(2016)

Sorry

I apologize
For

Hypotheticals

And soirées of
Questions
Low self-esteem
And

Doubt

It is not because I don't care
It is because I care so much

It is not because I want anything than
To be

PERFECT

S
O
R
R

Y

So many times you have forgiven me

I am in Eden

Purged of all my sin,
When you accept me as I am

(2016)

Portland

City upon a hill
Upon a river
Upon the rails

I took a drink of eternity
When I was within
Your
Tunnels

I found out what

I was

There

(2016)

Perfection

Anything less than perfection
Means
NOTHING
To me.

That is why I don't care about
Myself

The most wonderful nights have been
When I cried myself to sleep
For, it was then
That I had
The best of
Dreams.

If I could only go back
And change a few details

I know I would be

Happier

Because then, I would be

Perfection

Without those things
I am nothing
But a man trying to pass the time
Between
Depression cycles

I know people will call me selfish
But I am self-less
And I wish only to give way
To something better

The beautiful
Are *perfect*

Since I am not beautiful by living
I can only hope to be beautiful
In death

Perfection
Is all I want.

(2016)

That Night

Where are you now?
You were the man
I was in love with

You died
And I loved you even more

You live on in my
Memory

Where are you now?
What if you didn't really die?

Was it drugs?

I knew you were in pain

Now, I feel so guilty
For nothing giving you
Everything

(2016)

Bach

I hear your suites
In my head
How I wish I could
Playeverynote

Yet, I can't find the way
Because I cry
The moment I play
The simplest of
Chords

(2016)

Anorexia

I sing thy name my bod'ly muse! Beauty!
Bring to me my desired bod'ly shape
Make me beautiful to all who see me
I want to be perfection just for once
Because, being as I am is painful

(2016)

Do You Want A Ring?

Do you want a ring he asks
I smile because I do

Of course, I want
Der Ring des Nibelungen

I want to be a Valkyrie
And walk to meet my Siegfried

Of course, it's just a dream now
But

Dreams always come true

(2016)

Cotton Candy

Cotton Candy
Cotton Candy

I kiss your lips
So sweet
So soft
Like cotton candy

(2016)

It doesn't matter

At the end
We will be happy
And all the negative
Won't matter
Because
It doesn't matter

It never did

(2016)

Mimes

The timbre of the night
Is a beat
Gaining

Raising

W
  E
    W
      I
        L
          L

What can we do?

This may be

Something

Something

Nothing

Nothing?

Everything

(2016)

Boyfriends

I never expected
That we would be here now

So many more nights
Have we to spend like this

Eternity

People will say it's foolish to speak thus
But I say

What are we to prove
But by loving

Forever

(2016)

DMM

Beauty beauty wondrous beauty thou art
For I know not how to take the muse's part
And sing just how perfect you'll be to me
Since you are everything perfection can be

(2016)

Milky Way

Stars lighting up the sky
Making light between
Eternity

A starry sky is
Found

In the most isolated
Of places

(2016)

Postularum

In Natura
vertus est
Egohabeo
Causas mihi memora
Equus calibus

Musas
Musas

(2016)

Shylock

Venetian master
In the canals

The squares open up
And you a no longer
There

Where is Jessica now?
She is miles, miles away
Several leagues

I wish to know what
Happened to you

Venice
Was

You

(2016)

Othello

For you are great
You shall ever
Remain in our hearts

A man of honor
Never has surpassed you

Desdemona
Missed you
As

We too

Cyprus
Awaits you

(2016)

Notte

Questa notte
Voglio

È
È

Dove

Dove

Auitami

(2016)

When We Were Young

Happy was I
When it was all but dreams

Now, as I am here
In
Reality

I remember how much happier
It all was

I remember looking up
Into the stars
Wishing that this could be true

But now, it seems as tho it is
Relentlessly
Ennui

I remember sitting
Thinking about
Having this be true

How I wish it was anything else

When we were young
We could dream of anything

How I miss the dream
Instead
Of this reality

(2016)

Hāt

Heated streets
Sweat upon the front

A sip of warmed water

Dirt everywhere

The animals rush to sleep

As I

Labor on

(2016)

The Temple

We here the clarion
We hear the bells

Tolling
Tolling

Sounded
Sounded

SOUND THE ALARUM

we have no need

The temple is destroyèd

And we have nowhere

Left

(2016)

The King

Hail!
Hail!
Hail!
Hail my King

Lay thy men upon me
And kill me
To retain thine honor

(2016)

Saturday Night

L'homme ennuyé
Qui a entre dans
Ce monde

Pensez-vous que j'ai pas que
Ce moment

Ou peux je vous dire
Que

Non.

I just want to enter into this very world and
After seeing it so very
Filled

With emptiness

What was the point?

(2016)

Sunday Mornings

Sunday mornings are the
Best
And
Worst
Because there is little else to do but detest
everything about

Everything else

(2016)

The Corner of Fifth and Clément

N'avez vous écouté
Des portes fermées

What

Anyone would give

To

Be

A

Whore whore
Whore

(2016)

Debin

Jabotinsky was
Always telling us about
L'autre côté

Now we are here
Listening to these
Songs

Could we not find another place to be right now?
Because this
Side
Is

So many ages have passed since we held onto
A moment such as this.

Fleeting.

(2016)